PAUL REVERE'S RIDE

by
Henry Wadsworth Longfellow
illustrated by
Nancy Winslow Parker

Greenwillow Books, New York

To my ancestors both British and Colonial
who fought in the Revolutionary War

—*N. W. P.*

Library of Congress Cataloging in Publication Data

Longfellow, Henry Wadsworth, 1807–1882.
Paul Revere's ride.
Summary: The famous narrative poem recreating Paul
Revere's midnight ride in 1775 to warn the people of
the Boston countryside that the British were coming.
1. Revere, Paul, 1735–1818—Juvenile poetry.
2. Lexington, Battle of, 1775—Juvenile poetry.
3. Children's poetry, American.   [1. Revere, Paul, 1735–1818—Poetry.
2. Lexington, Battle of, 1775—Poetry.
3. Narrative poetry.   4. American poetry]
I. Parker, Nancy Winslow, ill.   II. Title.
PS2271.P3 1985   811'.3   84-4139
ISBN 0-688-04014-4   ISBN 0-688-04015-2 (lib. bdg.)

The British coat of arms which hung
in Boston until the American Revolution

THE SETTING

It was a windy, cold night in Boston on April 18, 1775. The city was overflowing with British troops sent by King George III to suppress the rebellious colonists. The soldiers camped in fields and commons in row upon row of white tents. The officers were billeted in private homes. Boston was in a state of siege, under curfew imposed by General Thomas Gage, commander of the British forces in America and Governor of Massachusetts.

General Gage knew that the local militia were stockpiling arms and ammunition in Concord. He also knew that the two leaders of the illegal Provincial Congress, John Hancock and Samuel Adams, were in Lexington. General Gage had orders from the King to arrest both men and ship them to England to stand trial. On this night, General Gage issued written orders to Colonel Francis Smith of the 10th Lincolnshires: "...You will march with the corps of grenadiers and light infantry put under your command with the utmost expedition and secrecy to Concord, where you will seize and destroy all the artillery and ammunition, provisions, tents, and all other military stores you find."

There were two routes out of Boston—one, across the neck by foot, called the "land" route; the other, by boat across the Charles River to the mainland, called the "sea" route.

Colonel Smith, with his second-in-command, Major Pitcairn of the Royal Marines, mustered eight companies of grenadiers, and eight companies of light infantry, totaling about seven hundred men. They moved quietly through the dark streets of Boston to the shore, boarded launches, and rowed to the mainland near Cambridge.

Paul Revere was a forty-year-old Boston silversmith whose business had suffered because of the difficulties with England. He turned his hand to producing revolutionary pamphlets and became an express rider-messenger for the revolutionary leaders; he also spied on British troop activity.

On this night, when Paul Revere discovered which route the British would take, he was to ride to Concord and warn the militia, waiting to move the military stores to a safer town.

Paul Revere's friend was John Pulling, sexton of the Old North Church. He was familiar with its layout and able to find doors and locks in the dark. It was Pulling who gave the famous signal, "One if by land, two if by sea," to Paul Revere, waiting across the bay. Pulling risked arrest and prison because he was breaking the curfew.

Paul Revere did not ride all the way to Concord as Longfellow would have us believe. He did arrive in Lexington, alerted the militia and helped Adams and Hancock escape capture. Then he started for Concord with two other men, but all three were captured by the British three miles outside Lexington. One of the men, Dr. Samuel Prescott, escaped in the dark and rode on to Concord with the news of the British advance.

These five men—a general, a silversmith, a sexton, a major, and a colonel— set the stage for the most famous day and year in American history: the 18th of April, 1775.

N. W. Parker
New York 1984

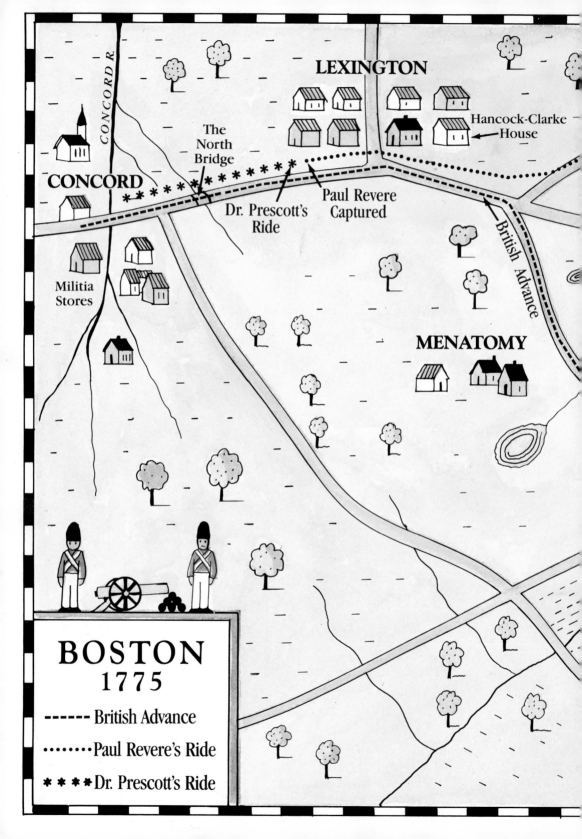

CONCORD R.

LEXINGTON

The
North
Bridge

Hancock-Clarke
House

CONCORD

Dr. Prescott's
Ride

Paul Revere
Captured

British Advance

Militia
Stores

MENATOMY

BOSTON
1775

- - - - - - British Advance

· · · · · · · · Paul Revere's Ride

✳ ✳ ✳ ✳ Dr. Prescott's Ride

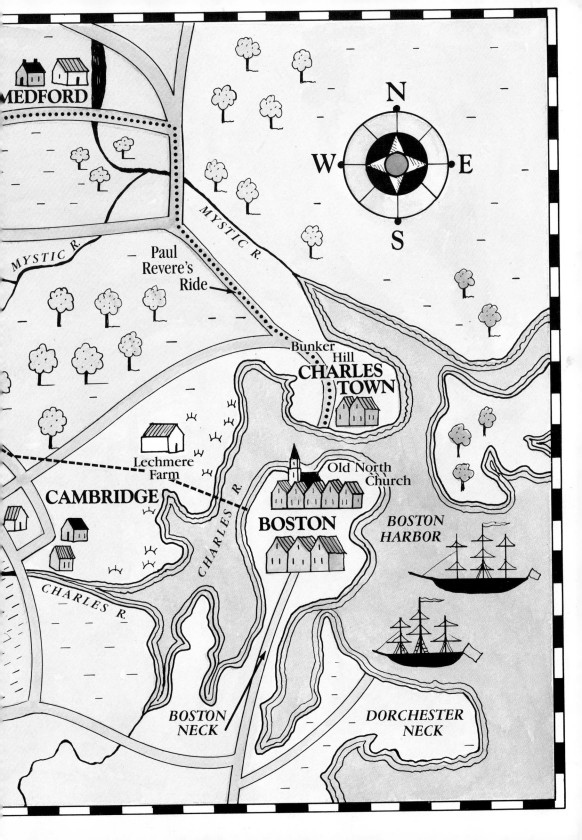

*Device attributed to Paul Revere,
showing skull and crossbones between
English crown and cap of liberty*

Listen, my children, and you shall hear
Of the midnight ride of Paul Revere,
On the eighteenth of April, in Seventy-five;
Hardly a man is now alive
Who remembers that famous day and year.

★HENRY WADSWORTH LONGFELLOW★

He said to his friend, "If the British march
By land or sea from the town tonight,
Hang a lantern aloft in the belfry arch
Of the North Church tower as a signal light,—

One, if by land, and two, if by sea;
And I on the opposite shore will be,
Ready to ride and spread the alarm
Through every Middlesex village and farm,
For the country-folk to be up and to arm."

Then he said, "Good night!" and with muffled oar
Silently rowed to the Charles Town shore,
Just as the moon rose over the bay,
Where swinging wide at her moorings lay
The Somerset, British man-of-war;

A phantom ship, with each mast and spar
Across the moon like a prison bar,
And a huge black hulk, that was magnified
By its own reflection in the tide.

Meanwhile, his friend, through alley and street,
Wanders and watches with eager ears,
Till in silence around him he hears
The muster of men at the barrack door,

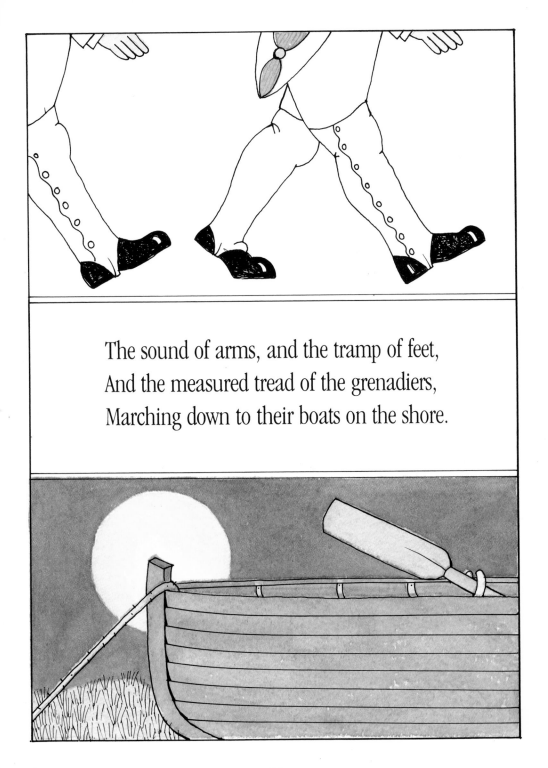

The sound of arms, and the tramp of feet,
And the measured tread of the grenadiers,
Marching down to their boats on the shore.

Then he climbed to the tower of the church,
Up the wooden stairs, with stealthy tread,
To the belfry-chamber overhead,
And startled the pigeons from their perch
On the sombre rafters, that round him made
Masses and moving shapes of shade,—

Up the trembling ladder, steep and tall,
To the highest window in the wall,
Where he paused to listen and look down
A moment on the roofs of the town,
And the moonlight flowing over all.

Beneath, in the churchyard, lay the dead,
In their night-encampment on the hill,
Wrapped in silence so deep and still
That he could hear, like a sentinel's tread,
The watchful night-wind, as it went
Creeping along from tent to tent,
And seeming to whisper, "All is well!"

A moment only he feels the spell
Of the place and the hour, and the secret dread
Of the lonely belfry and the dead;

For suddenly all his thoughts are bent
On a shadowy something far away,
Where the river widens to meet the bay,—

A line of black that bends and floats
On the rising tide, like a bridge of boats.

Meanwhile, impatient to mount and ride,
Booted and spurred, with a heavy stride
On the opposite shore walked Paul Revere.

Now he patted his horse's side,
Now gazed at the landscape far and near,

Then, impetuous, stamped the earth,
And turned and tightened his saddle-girth;

But mostly he watched with eager search
The belfry-tower of the Old North Church,
As it rose above the graves on the hill,
Lonely and spectral and sombre and still.

And lo! as he looks, on the belfry's height
A glimmer, and then a gleam of light!

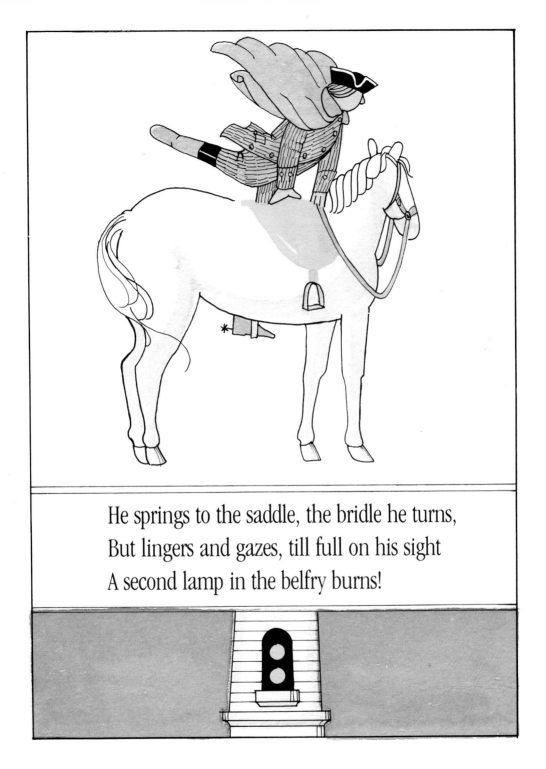

He springs to the saddle, the bridle he turns,
But lingers and gazes, till full on his sight
A second lamp in the belfry burns!

A hurry of hoofs in a village street,
A shape in the moonlight, a bulk in the dark,
And beneath, from the pebbles, in passing, a spark
Struck out by a steed flying fearless and fleet;

That was all! And yet, through the gloom and the
    light,
The fate of a nation was riding that night;
And the spark struck out by that steed, in his flight,
Kindled the land into flame with its heat.

He has left the village and mounted the steep,
And beneath him, tranquil and broad and deep,
Is the Mystic, meeting the ocean tides;

And under the alders, that skirt its edge,
Now soft on the sand, now loud on the ledge,
Is heard the tramp of his steed as he rides.

It was twelve by the village clock
When he crossed the bridge into Medford town.
He heard the crowing of the cock,

And the barking of the farmer's dog,
And felt the damp of the river fog,
That rises after the sun goes down.

It was one by the village clock,
When he galloped into Lexington.
He saw the gilded weathercock
Swim in the moonlight as he passed,

And the meeting-house windows, blank and bare,
Gaze at him with a spectral glare,
As if they already stood aghast
At the bloody work they would look upon.

It was two by the village clock,
When he came to the bridge in Concord town.
He heard the bleating of the flock,

And the twitter of birds among the trees,
And felt the breath of the morning breeze
Blowing over the meadows brown.

And one was safe and asleep in his bed
Who at the bridge would be first to fall,
Who that day would be lying dead,
Pierced by a British musket-ball.

You know the rest. In the books you have read,
How the British Regulars fired and fled,—

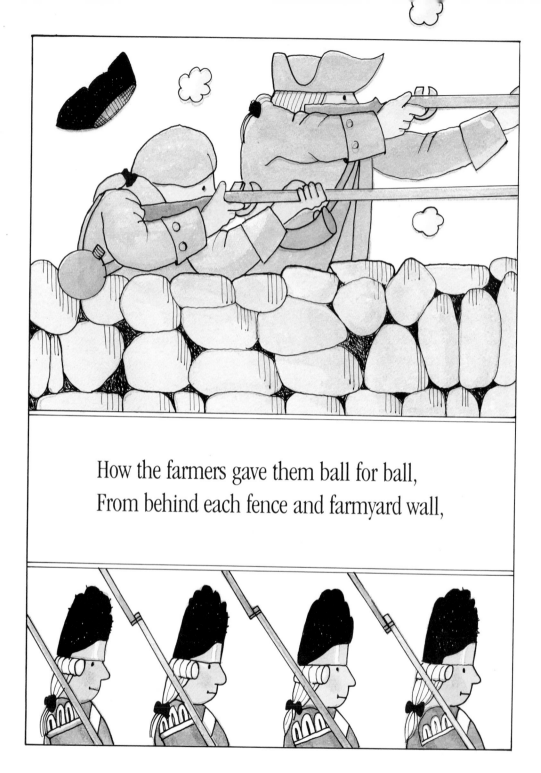

How the farmers gave them ball for ball,
From behind each fence and farmyard wall,

Chasing the red-coats down the lane,
Then crossing the fields to emerge again
Under the trees at the turn of the road,
And only pausing to fire and load.

So through the night rode Paul Revere;
And so through the night went his cry of alarm
To every Middlesex village and farm,—

A cry of defiance and not of fear,
A voice in the darkness, a knock at the door,
And a word that shall echo forever-more!

For, borne on the night-wind of the Past,
Through all our history, to the last,
in the hour of darkness and peril and need,

1775

1812

1917

The people will waken and listen to hear
The hurrying hoof-beats of that steed,
And the midnight message of Paul Revere.

Geographical and Military Notes

ALDER—A shrub or tree which likes to grow by riverbanks. It is found in northern states and colder regions.

BELFRY—The part of a church steeple where the bell is hung.

BRIDGE—The now famous North Bridge in Concord, Massachusetts, where a small company of militia fired on the stunned British troops. A brief battle ensued where many militiamen fell.

BRITISH REGULARS, RED-COATS—The King's troops. They wore scarlet coats, white pants, white leggings, and white vests.

CHARLES TOWN—Situated across the harbor from Boston, Charles Town was settled in 1628, and by the time of Paul Revere's ride, had grown to 2800 people. The British set fire to the town during the Battle of Bunker Hill (June 17, 1775) by firing hot shot from British warships in Boston Harbor.

CONCORD—A town about seventeen miles northwest of Boston where the militia had stored arms and ammunition.

ENCAMPMENT—A military base consisting of rows of white army tents pitched on a village green or farmer's field in Revolutionary America.

GRENADIERS—One of the out-flank companies of every British regiment. They are big, powerful men: the elite of the army. They march ahead of the troops and toss grenades. Their tall, brimless, bearskin hats do not get in the way when they throw grenades. Although grenades were not used during the American Revolution, the grenadiers wore the hats to appear even taller than they were.

LEXINGTON—A town about eleven miles northwest of Boston.

LIGHT INFANTRY—A company of men in every British regiment known for its intelligence and its ability to strike swiftly and move rapidly.

MAN-OF-WAR—A warship.

MEDFORD TOWN—A town about five miles north of Boston.

MEETING-HOUSE—A colonial name for a house of worship.

MIDDLESEX—A county in Eastern Massachusetts which included the towns of Medford, Lexington, and Concord.

MUSKET-BALL—Musket ammunition. When the ball was fired, it went only one hundred yards and then fell harmless to the ground. The musket was more effective as a mount for the bayonet.

MYSTIC—The Mystic River which flows north of Boston.

REGIMENT—A British regiment of foot in 1775 consisted of about 477 men, comprised of eight companies of foot soldiers, and one each of grenadier and infantry companies.

SADDLE-GIRTH—The band which goes under the horse's belly to hold the saddle in place, and which fastens under the saddle flaps.

*The Great Seal
of the United States
from the original die
of 1782*